LESSONS FROM GRIMM:
How to Write a Fairy Tale
High School Workbook (Grades 9-12)

Shonna Slayton

AMARETTO PRESS

Ordering Information: Special discounts are available on quantity purchases by corporations, associations, and others. For details, contact the author at the web address above.

Cover design © Seedlings Design Studio
Interior design © SaRose Design

Paperback ISBN: 978-1-947736-06-1

Amaretto Press
Phoenix, AZ

Other Books by Shonna Slayton

Nonfiction

Lessons From Grimm: How To Write a Fairy Tale

Lessons From Grimm: How to Write a Fairy Tale (workbook series)

Writing Prompts From Grimm: A fairy-tale themed workbook for Grades 3-6

Writing Prompts From Grimm: A fairy-tale themed workbook for Grades 7-12

Fiction

Fairy-tale Inheritance Series

Cinderella's Dress

Cinderella's Shoes

Cinderella's Legacy

Snow White's Mirror

Beauty's Rose

The Little Mermaid (coming soon)

Lost Fairy Tales Series

The Tower Princess

Historical Women

Liz and Nellie: Nellie Bly and Elizabeth Bisland's Race Around the World in Eighty Days

Table of Contents

Introduction

THE PATTERN

When Grimms' fairy tales are boiled down to their simplest components, we have a pattern. This workbook uses that pattern to walk you through writing a fairy tale:

» Once upon a time
» there was a character
» who lived in a setting
» and had a problem (plot).
» Fairy tale magic intervened/interfered
» and everyone learned a lesson (theme).

How to Use This Workbook

This workbook is based off of the text *Lessons from Grimm: How to Write a Fairy Tale*. Some of that text has been repeated here in simplified format. To delve further into the concepts, be sure to get the book.

Section 1: Find Your Fairy Tale Voice

We're going to start building your fairy tale voice by pinpointing all the components you enjoy the most about fairy tales. In this first section, you'll analyze your favorite characters, settings, plots, and themes.

Here, you'll compile your personal lists of archetypes and tropes. Highlight what catches your attention in the samples and add your own favorites into the spaces provided. You can find the complete lists in the Appendix section of *Lessons from Grimm*. If you are more visual, use the space to scrapbook what inspires you.

Section 2: Brainstorm Your Fairy Tale

You'll be using this space to make notes about your fairy tale. You'll be given space to work out your chosen characters, settings, plots, themes, and fairy tale magic.

SECTION 1: FIND YOUR FAIRY TALE VOICE

Before I started writing fairy tales, I had a definite opinion of what a fairy tale ought to be. I thought a fairy tale should include a princess, a fairy, and a bit of magic. Simple, right? But not too far into studying Grimms' tales, I had to change my opinion.

Surprisingly, even though their stories are called fairy tales, there are no fairies. Nor are there any fairy godmothers. Instead, the Grimms write of wise women who have magical abilities that they use for good. And would it surprise you, like it did me, that there are very few dragons in Grimm? And what about those decidedly scary stories which seem to be more akin to horror stories than fairy tales? There are also a number of religious tales found in Grimm.

What alerts a reader to a fairy tale is a combination of all the parts we're going to look at, beginning with genre. Genre provides the foundation on which to build a fairy tale.

Before reading on, stop and think about your favorite fairy tales and see if you can pinpoint what kind of fairy tale you like best.

Do you lean toward princess stories?

Dragons?

Fairy godmothers?

Or do you hope to read about strange ghostly creatures who come out at night? Stories about young men going out to make their way in the world? Tales with clever soldiers or clueless giants?

Throughout this book, we'll be pulling from recurring patterns. Tropes. Archetypes. The elements that make a fairy tale a fairy tale.

Dictionary.com defines a trope as any literary or rhetorical device, [such] as metaphor, metonymy, synecdoche, and irony, that consists in the use of words in other than their literal sense. Or, more simplified from Merriam-Webster.com: a common or overused theme or device. Cliché. And an archetype is defined at Dictionary.com as the original pattern or model from which all things of the same kind are copied or on which they are based; a model or first form; prototype.

There was a ... *CHARACTER*

"There was once on a time a poor man, who could no longer support his only son."

"There was once a girl who was idle and would not spin, and let her mother say what she would, she could not bring her to it."

"There were once on a time a king and a queen who lived happily together and had twelve children, but they were all boys."

A poor man. A son. A girl. A mother. A king and a queen. Twelve brothers. The Grimm stories are about all kinds of people. From peasants to kings. From murderers to priests. Not to mention imaginative creatures like giants, elves, and water nixies.

In fairy tales, there are few limits on who we can create. Our characters don't necessarily have to look or act a certain way. A girl can have impossibly long hair, or a man can turn into a lion during the day.

Grimms' characters have a variety of occupations, physical descriptions, and family situations.

But these are all external characteristics.

What attracts readers to care deeply about fairy tale characters is a shared emotional experience. We might not know what it's like to be locked in a tower from childhood, but we've all felt loneliness. We can relate to the hope of looking out through an open window and wondering what's out there for us. We don't take the form of a lion during the day, but we know what it feels like to be different from those around us and not quite belong.

Even though the Grimm stories often lack emotional cues, readers still reach into the circumstances with their own feelings. We imagine what the characters are going through. We instinctively know it's those deep emotions that cause characters to act. And we wonder what we would do in those circumstances.

Go through this sampling of characters pulled from Grimms' stories and circle/highlight the ones that stand out to you. Then, add your own favorites. Use the space to expand the descriptions to include your favorite traits, descriptions, names, etc. Remember, you're building your fairy tale voice. How you handle character is one element of your voice.

Characters

apprentice

artisan, astronomer

beautiful, haughty princess

beggar

broom-maker

brothers

burgomaster

chamber maid

charcoal-burner

child's nurse

coachman

cook

court-shoemaker

cup-bearer

daughter of an innkeeper

daughter, never laughed

discharged soldier

drummer

faithful servant

ferryman

fiddler

fisherman

foster father

gardener

godfather

godmother

goldsmith

goose girl

helpful maiden

huntsman

hussar

innkeeper

jam seller

judge

king

king's armor-bearer

king's council

knight

locksmith

lord

magician

maid

merchant

miller's wife

musician

orphan

overly confident prince

page

peasant

poor farmer

poor man and woman

poor tailor

poor woodcutter

prince

princess

queen

robber

sentry

servant

shapeshifter thief

stepmother who is a witch

stepsister

swineherd's daughter

tailor

thief

trusted servants

waiting-maid

watchman by the gates

widow

wood cutter

Fairy Tale Characters

bird that grants wishes

changeling

Death

dragon

dwarfs/mannikins

elves

fox with nine tails

frog that prophesies

giants

gold chickens

golden bird

griffin

imp

lion who always tells the truth

nixie

thumbling

unicorn

wise woman (fairy godmother)

People Enchanted and Turned Into

ant

bear

bull

cat

church

chandelier

cow

donkey

dove

dragon

duck

eagle

fish

fishpond

flower

fox

frog

half hedgehog

hen

lake

lion

nightingale

old man

poodle

raven

red stone landmark

rooster

rose-tree

rose

sea-hare

stag

stone

swan

toad

tree

whale

white horse

wood

Positive Traits

beautiful

compassionate

courageous

curious

fair of face

faithful

fearless

good and honorable

good heart

handsome

honest

joyous

kind

merry

old

pious and good

poor

silly

strong

wise

young

Negative Traits

bad heart

black of heart

crafty

cunning

deceitful

drunken

envious heart

evil-hearted

faithless

false

greedy

hard-hearted

haughty

hearts of stone

idle

liar

mocking

negligent

proud

stubborn

thief

vile

wicked

Add your own characters and traits:

Who lived in a ... *Setting*

Settings in Grimms' fairy tales are not elaborate, but are often essential to the story. If you hear the words castle and dark forest, your mind is already walking that winding path into a fairy tale. And that's with only three words! Imagine how enticing the tale will be as you develop a rich setting for your fairy tale backdrop.

For modern fairy tale writers, setting goes a long way in creating that once-upon-a-time feeling, and you'll want to spend more time establishing setting than the Grimms did.

Often, settings can become characters themselves, or they can have a transformative part in the plot or character development.

Go through this list of settings found in Grimms' fairy tales and highlight the ones that interest you:

Settings
ballroom
bedroom
bridge
carriage
castle
cottage in the woods,
forest
fork in the road
glass mountain
hut in the forest
inn
kitchen
lake
meadow
mill
murderer's den
pasture

pigeon house
ravine
river/river bank
road
robber's den
sea
stable
tower
town hung with black crape
waste place
well: portal to another world

Types of Trees
apple tree
aspen tree
fir tree
hazel bush
hollow tree
juniper tree

oak
old lime tree
pear tree
rose-tree,
trees of gold, silver, and diamonds
tree with a door

Timing
at midnight
daybreak
full moon
middle of winter
six o'clock
sunrise
two o'clock
three days
seven days
seven years

Add your own settings:

AND HAD A PROBLEM ... *PLOT*

In Grimms' fairy tales, plot is often random and quirky—three women are changed into flowers which grow in a field, but one of them is allowed to go home at night *(A Riddling Tale)*. Sometimes, the plots are on-the-nose specific—a traveler saves groups of ants, ducks and bees, and then later on, he needs the specific skills of the ants, ducks, and bees who then come to his aid *(The Queen Bee)*.

But overall, what marks Grimms' fairy tales is trouble, trouble, and more trouble. The stakes are personal for our fairy tale characters. The entire world might not be saved when a young man finds a wishing saddle, but an enchanted princess *can* be.

Side note: Do you know if you are writing a retelling or an adaptation? Here is how I look at retellings and adaptations:

Retelling: recreating the fairy tale. You are following the same basic plot with the same characters, filling in the gaps of the original tale, providing more atmosphere to the setting, and adding motivation to the characters. But in essence, the fairy tale is the same as the original. It's been retold.

Adaptation: more of an inspired-by tale. You are taking elements from the tale and creating a more original story. A reader may or may not even recognize it's an adaptation unless it's pointed out to them. It's been adapted.

Go through this list of plots found in Grimms' fairy tales and highlight the ones that interest you:

- » after long wishing and praying for a child, one is born
- » animals reveal the antagonist
- » antagonist dresses in disguise as a peddler-woman
- » arrested protagonist is given a chance to redeem himself by going to another kingdom to steal something from there
- » assumptions lead to misunderstandings
- » break the rule and be kicked out of paradise
- » brother avenges brothers who have been swindled
- » brother kills brother to claim the reward

- » brothers steal what youngest brother obtained and act like they did the work
- » challenge to find the lost gold crown, missing since ancient times
- » contest to claim an inheritance
- » contest to marry a princess
- » deathbed promises
- » eating the forbidden fruit/food/opening the forbidden door brings severe consequences
- » faced with poverty and hunger, brothers set off into the world to seek their fortune
- » faithful servant sacrifices himself to save the king
- » false queen: murder the queen and put an imposter in her place, magically transformed but for one telltale sign that must be hidden
- » find a lost object
- » hide out in the woods while their lives are in danger
- » king has a feast, inviting all the bachelors in the country in order to find a husband for the princess
- » king manipulates his children but they thwart him in the end
- » king tracks down his wife who had been sent into hiding after word came that he (falsely) wanted her killed
- » lovers are separated, injured, yet find one another again
- » make a rash vow of revenge only to reverse it and protect the one you vowed to kill
- » man risks death to try to answer riddle and marry the princess
- » naive traveler gets swindled at an inn
- » old woman gives an invisibility cloak
- » pass a series of tests to get something from the king
- » plot a kidnapping
- » prince or princess travels to a distant kingdom
- » princess chooses to live as a commoner instead of marry someone she doesn't want to marry
- » princess disguises herself as kitchen maid.
- » princess forced to marry an evil man in order to bring peace
- » princess gives suitors sleeping draughts so they can't learn her secrets
- » princess is blackmailed against speaking the truth

- » queen hears someone crying and upon learning (falsely) the reason, sees opportunity and brings her home to meet her son
- » riddle to be solved
- » rival kills the rescuer while he sleeps
- » royalty pretending to be working class
- » see what is behind a locked door and life is changed
- » servant is suspected of stealing when he is innocent and sets out to prove it
- » servant sent in place of the royal
- » servant tries to cover up their own misdeed by lying to the other
- » shunned wise woman curses a baby in order to hurt the parents
- » someone is recognized because of a ring
- » stepmother relentlessly hunts down stepchild(ren) to kill them
- » suitors put to death if they fail the test
- » talking animals are often enchanted people
- » three sons compete for the kingdom by bringing home a series of "the most beautiful _____"
- » three tasks to break an enchantment are inscribed on stone table
- » three wishes gone wrong
- » true bride has to prove who she is
- » true bridegroom sneaks back into town the day before the wedding and sets up in the inn
- » use an invisibility cloak to learn a secret
- » victim of rumors
- » warned not to eat or drink, travelers take the advice and someone else gets poisoned
- » while a queen sleeps, her baby is stolen and she is blamed for it
- » widower marries a woman who has ulterior motives
- » wise women bestow gifts on a baby
- » youngest daughter accepts marriage proposal from unpopular man who later comes back a fine man

Magic intervenes/interferes

Since magic is a known staple in the fairy tale genre, I was surprised to learn that there are not as many magical tales in Grimm as I expected. And the magic is somewhat... squishy. Hard to pin down.

What makes fairy tale magic different from other literary types of magic? In our outline I say "magic intervenes," and by that I don't mean that magic solved the character's problems. Fairy tale magic often kicks things off, by enchanting someone in the backstory, for example, or it can provide a tool for the hero.

Go through this list of magic found in Grimms' fairy tales and highlight the ones that interest you:

» backpack contains whatever is wished for inside
» ball of yarn will unroll to reveal a hidden path
» bone carved into a horn sings the song of the person's murder
» cabbage that when eaten turns the person into a donkey; another cabbage turns them back into a human
» dwarf ring that allows you to control air spirits
» fiddle that draws people close or makes them dance
» gold bird: feathers made of gold, eggs of solid gold
» gold horse - runs faster than the wind
» handkerchief with three drops of mother's blood gives princess protection
» healing apples
» healing leaves
» healing water
» horn: blows down all the walls and fortifications
» invisibility cloak
» leaves restore life
» looking-glass which speaks the truth
» needle that can sew anything together seamlessly
» purse that never runs out of money

- » ring that gives wearer strength
- » sleeping potion
- » telescope that can see everything in heaven and earth
- » tree of golden fruit that only allows its owner to pick it
- » walnuts that hold beautiful dresses
- » wand to open doors
- » wand turns people into objects, stone
- » well that turns everything that touches its water to gold
- » wishing saddle, boots, cap, cloak or ring will take you where you wish to be
- » wishing table or wishing cloth covers itself with food when you command it

Add your own fairy tale magic:

And Everyone Learned . . . *Theme*

Theme can be a hard concept to wrap your mind around. Sometimes you won't know the theme until you've written the story and then look back at it. If you have trouble pinning down a theme, think about it this way: What do the characters—and vicariously, the readers—learn the most? This is the main theme. And if you can discover your main theme, you can focus the story around that theme so everything taken together: the genre, the characters, the setting, the plot, the magic—all of it—becomes more impactful.

One general theme is that fairy tales are allegories for growing up. We are reading about the transition of a child through puberty and into adulthood. This is especially so in the stories where a child leaves home, encounters adversity, and overcomes it.

Some authors like to use one-word themes which can give you a general category of theme to work with. But if you dig deeper, you'll uncover the specific lesson about that general category. For example, the theme of *love* is pretty general, but *love conquers all* says something specific about love.

Go through this list of themes found in Grimms' fairy tales and highlight the ones that interest you:

GENERAL THEME . . . . SPECIFIC THEME

General Theme	Specific Theme
anger	misplaced anger leads to foolish action
appearances	do not judge others on their appearances
assumptions	assumptions lead to misunderstandings
bravery	don't sit idly by when you can stop a menace
commitment	stay true and you'll be rewarded in the end
confidence	boldness will be rewarded
courage	try even though others have failed
deception	deception leads to downfall
deception	don't try to be someone you're not
envy	envy leads to hatred
envy	envy makes a person miserable
faith	having faith will allow you to complete any task

family	sisters can be relied upon to keep the family together
family	the greatest reward is having a family
fear	fear is best met with bravery and courage
gratitude	you appreciate what you had when it's gone
greed	greed leads to dishonest behavior
helping others	protect the innocent
honor	the honorable will be restored
humility	acting with humility gains respect
humility	embrace humility and you can make the world better
integrity	doing what you say you will do brings honor
jealousy	jealousy becomes all-consuming
justice	people get their just reward in the end
kindness	be kind to people and animals alike
love	love is patient and waits
love	love is worth fighting for
love	love seeks the good for others
love	true loves will find each other after a separation
loyalty	stay true and you'll be rewarded
magic	can be used for good or evil
motherly love	a mother protects her children
perseverance	be patient in affliction; things will get better
perseverance	never give up on your goal
power	ultimate power corrupts
pride	a proud spirit will be humbled
pride	boasting leads to trouble
pride	pride leads to destruction
repentance	repentance brings restoration
respect	treat others with respect
safety	beware of someone who is too controlling
trust	trust but verify
truth	truth wins in the end
wisdom	don't make a contract without first knowing all the details
work ethic	diligent work is rewarded

How to Stand out: A Touch of Whimsy

What makes a fairy tale *feel* like a fairy tale?

Much of it comes down to the idea of whimsy. Dictionary.com defines whimsy as *anything odd or fanciful; a product of playful or capricious fancy.*

Grimms' fairy tales are often short and to the point, no-nonsense in their approach. But every so often, the Grimms throw in a glimmer of whimsy. It's usually in the magic, but can also be found in the characters, the setting, the plot. Anything that catches your reader off guard in a quirky way: A woman with a large thumb, a mountain made of glass, or a challenge to pluck a feather off a griffin. Spinning straw into gold, using a girl's braided hair to climb a tower, or putting a gold collar on the neck of a boy-turned-into-a-roebuck to lead him around.

Earlier, we defined trope as *any literary or rhetorical device, as metaphor, metonymy, synecdoche, and irony, that consists in the use of words in other than their literal sense.* In fairy tales, you can lean heavily into these rhetorical devices when you're looking to add whimsy.

Make notes here about your favorite whimsical fairy tale examples.

SECTION 2: BRAINSTORM YOUR OWN FAIRY TALE

CHARACTER

Now that you've thought about all the things you love in a fairy tale, start brainstorming your own story. Refer back to your favorites lists when you need inspiration. Feel free to jump around to the different sections as you come up with ideas. You'll have space for making notes on characters, settings, plots, fairy tale magic, and theme.

CHARACTER OUTLINES:

Protagonist (main character)

Choose from your list of favorite characters in section one. You'll start with an archetype (princess in a tower, unloved stepchild, youngest prince), then build a full-fledged character.

Here you'll find space to write about the character's physical features, but more important than those is to focus on the internal aspects of the character and how they relate to the plot.

Goals: The protagonist ought to have a goal strong enough to sustain the length of the short story or novel.

Motivation/Need: Their motivation has to make sense as they work toward fulfilling that goal.

Conflict: The person or circumstances getting in the way of the character realizing their goal.

Stakes: What is at stake for a character in a fairy tale is generally small compared with, say, a superhero movie where the future of the entire world is at stake. In a fairy tale, the stakes are more personal. It's often the protagonist's way of life that's at stake. Sometimes her kingdom. Or, the most personal of all, her own life. Because stakes are so important to have, yet often difficult to define, I've put them at the top of the brainstorming lists as a reminder to keep the stakes at the forefront of your story.

You might be thinking that some of these "characteristics" are more related to plot. Character is intertwined with plot, so while you're thinking about the internal life of your character, it's important to consider *why* your characters are the way they are.

Let's look at Cinderella as an example:

Cinderella

As Cinderella's mother is dying, she admonishes the child to "be good and pious, and then the good God will always protect you." The next year, Cinderella's father remarries and the new step family quickly turns her into a servant. Her father is distant, but still living in the house. He describes Cinderella as "a little stunted kitchen-wench which my late wife left behind her." (If you are only familiar with Disney's version, based largely on Perrault's, you'll want to read Grimms', which is quite different.) Life can't get much worse for Cinderella, yet she remains good and pious like her mother told her to. The hazel twig she plants grows into a tree and the bird living in it gives her whatever she requests. Cinderella's past experiences give her the motivation to better her circumstances. When an opportunity arises (the three-day festival for the prince to choose a bride) she is prepared to make the most of it.

Stakes: a future of degrading servitude to her family

Goal: to escape her situation, if only for the festival

Motivation/Need: she's been loved before (by her mother) so she knows she should be valued more than she currently is

Conflict: her family is against her at every turn

Start brainstorming your own protagonist.

Name:

Stakes:

Goal:

Motivation/Need:

Conflict:

Personal History:

Physical Characteristics:

Other Notes

Like the protagonist, the antagonist ought to have a personal interest in the story.

The Singing Bone

A wild boar is terrorizing the kingdom. The king offers his daughter's hand in marriage to the man who kills the boar. Two brothers set off to kill the boar, the youngest getting a special spear from a dwarf. It works! The youngest returns with the boar, first stopping to celebrate with his brother. But his brother is wicked and wants the glory for himself.

Antagonist: the older brother

Stakes: future as a prince

Goal: to kill a wild boar and win the hand of the princess

Motivation: pride

Conflict: he has to thwart his own brother

Start brainstorming your own antagonist.

Name:

Stakes:

Goal:

Motivation/Need:

Conflict:

Personal History:

Physical Characteristics:

Other Notes:

Side Characters

Most of the time we focus on the main characters in the story, but side characters, secondary characters, or sidekicks can add a lot of life to a story. Whether they're bringing comic relief or a plot twist, we love our side characters.

Use this space to list your side characters and the ways they will influence the plot. Consider the role of fairy tale characters like Grimms' wise women (fairy godmothers) and mentors who give magical gifts.

SETTING

Use this space to make notes on your setting and how it can affect the story. Here are some exercises to get you thinking about setting.

1. List at least three elements of setting that are important to your fairy tale. Consider natural landscape, architecture, climate.

2. For each of those elements, brainstorm a list of descriptive words you can use when your characters are moving in that setting. Think of it like creating a palette, much like an artist would for a painting. Employ all of your character's senses: sight, sound, hearing, taste, smell, intuition. Come up with some fairy-tale-like descriptions, adding a touch of whimsy.

3. Create a story board for your setting. Attach images, sketch important backgrounds, or draw a map.

4. How can you use your setting to create atmosphere in your story?

5. Find three important moments in your story to add atmosphere to heighten the moment.

Make notes on your setting.

TROPES

As you read through the Grimm stories, you'll notice similarities in several plots. The orphaned girl mistreated by her stepmother. A sister saving her brothers. A barren woman praying for a child. You can use these common plot patterns to quickly form the basis of your own fairy tale.

The most popular fairy tales involve royalty and romance with a good dose of palace intrigue. Think about Cinderella, Sleeping Beauty, and Snow-White.

A common fairy tale trope is for a Father to Give Away his Daughter in Marriage to a man who can Perform an Extraordinary Feat: Kill the Beast Terrorizing the land (The Two Brothers) Find a Lost Object (The Queen Bee) Or, as a Reward for Kindness. (Bearskin)

Sometimes, the princess is okay with this arrangement.

Sometimes, she talks her father into making the man do yet another extraordinary feat in the hopes that he fails and she doesn't have to marry him (The White Snake).

Or, as in the case of The Skillful Huntsman, she can be a princess who outright Refuses to Marry the man who claims to have defeated the giants who were after her. Instead, she may Give up her Family Title and go off to Earn her Own Living.

You can combine tropes to come up with an original tale.

TEST OF THREE

The plot device of rule of three is a standard story-telling technique. In Grimms' fairy tales, we often see this technique applied to various tests a character might go through.

1. **Morality Test**: Various challenges are placed before the character to see what he or she is made of. Will they make the moral choice? The alternative to the moral choice is usually to act selfishly and is demonstrated by those who fail the test. Those who pass, get the reward.

2. **Inheritance Test**: Brother is pitted against brother to see who should win the inheritance. Usually there is only one winner, but one story in Grimm turns the test on its head and the brothers share the inheritance.

3. **Marry-the-Princess Test**: Either the king or the princess herself devises dangerous or impossible challenges for prospective suitors to undergo. The king is trying to find the very best for his daughter, but if she's got a hand in the rules, it's often because she's not interested in marrying.

ROMANCE IN FAIRY TALES

When people hear fairy tale, they think about romance. A prince and a princess. The Royalty Tales. Some tales are more romantic than others, and these romantic tales remain the most popular with readers today, especially in stories aimed at teens and young adults.

In this section, we'll zero in on what makes romance so special in Grimms' fairy tales.

Romantic Settings

Even though Grimms' tales are not overtly descriptive, they evoke romantic settings. We're talking fairy tale kingdoms, castles, and walks through the forest. Romance blossoms near ponds and under linden trees. A briar hedge parts to let the right prince through at the right time. In several tales we read about a series of balls where the women are wearing beautiful dresses each night. And in an epic fairy tale we see a woman travel all the way to the sun, moon, and stars to find her love.

Romantic Characters

Sacrificial love plays out over and over in fairy tales. There is something admirable about a character who has someone else's best interests at heart:

- A woman gives up her life during the day to be with a man who is a prince in human form only at night, but a lion by day.

- A man risks his life to battle a dragon to save a princess and her kingdom.

Ultimately, romance in a fairy tale favors the kind, humble, and pure of heart. In a world marred by evil intentions, these characters rise above, and we root for them.

Women are beautiful, their outside appearance a reflection of their inner beauty and strength of character. Men are courageous, having passed various tests to prove their worth. Together, their relationship works because readers intuitively feel that their union is one of like souls.

Again, when creating characters, think in extremes. Fairy tale characters are either extremely poor or extremely wealthy. They are the poor miller's daughter, or the princess. The poor, discharged soldier or the king.

Couples can then be made from the extremes, as long as their inner characters are compatible. A man can be a humble farmer with a noble character, and that makes him worthy of the princess.

The romantic plot follows the outward journey of the two people, as well as their inner journeys that take place, bringing down those barriers and allowing the couple to finally be together. For example, there are several fairy tales where the royal figure needs to be humbled before he or she finds love.

Romantic (Grand) Gestures

The grand gesture in a fairy tale is often very grand indeed. In romance novels, when one character sacrifices something for the other to let them know how much they are loved, we call this a grand gesture. Typically, the grand gesture occurs near the end of the story.

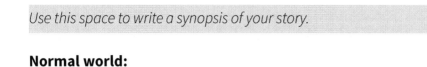

Normal world:

Show protagonist confronting a problem in regular world.

The inciting incident:

Explain what starts the story rolling; what sets up some mystery and foreshadows the beginnings of conflict.

First plot point:

Point of no return; the main character cannot go back to the way things were, they have to keep going forward until things are resolved.

Rising stakes:

List some problems and questions that propel us to keep reading: How will they survive and attain their goal?

Midpoint:

What is the midpoint reversal or reveal?

Dark moment:

Describe how things have never been worse for the protagonist

Second plot point:

This is the final "things set in motion" major plot point.

Climax and conclusion:

Describe how the loose ends are tied up.

PLOT CHART

Map out key scenes here

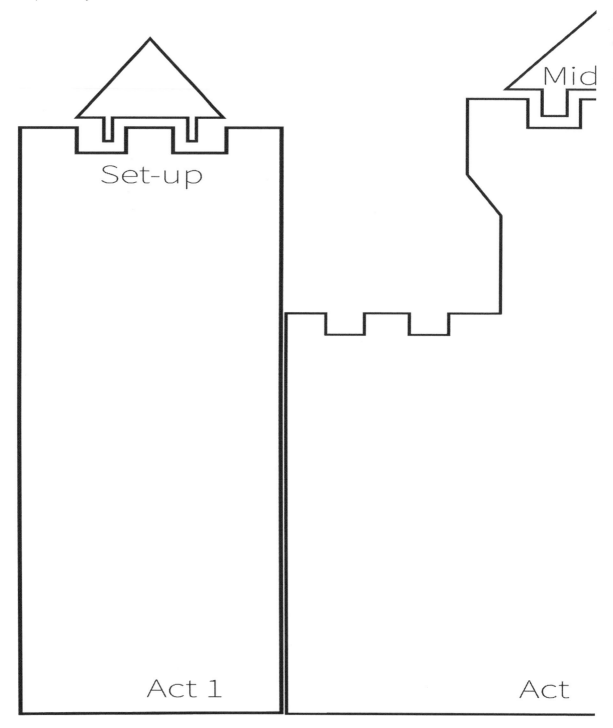

Set-up

Act 1

Mid

Act

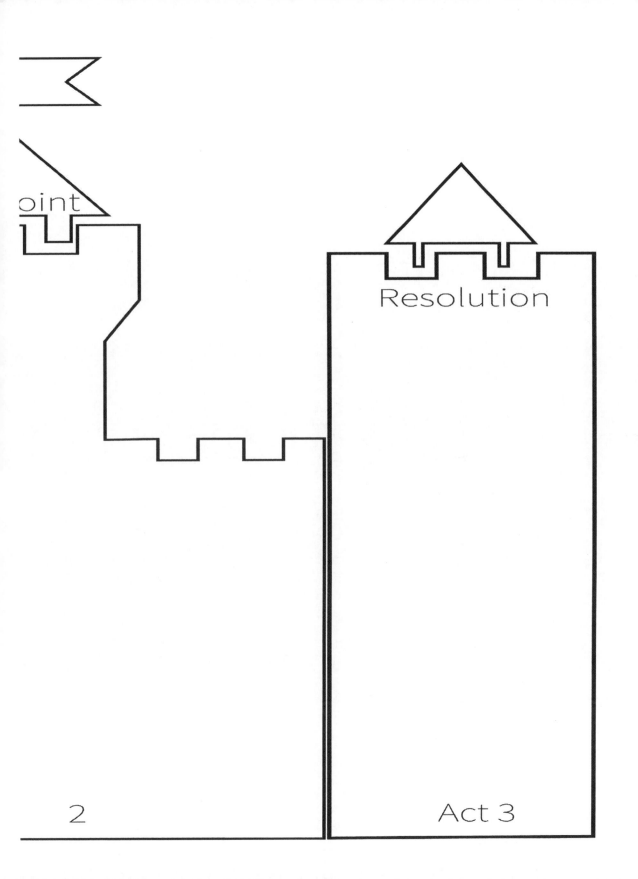

oint

Resolution

Act 3

ESCALATION: HOW TO MAKE THINGS WORSE

1. Track where your fairy tale escalates the tension. Can you add more tension?

2. Has the protagonist been confronted with an Impossible Bargain/Choice?

3. Aside from escalating major plot points, what are some ways you can add micro-tension to escalate a scene?

4. What is the communication like in the story? What happens when you change the plot by twisting a message?

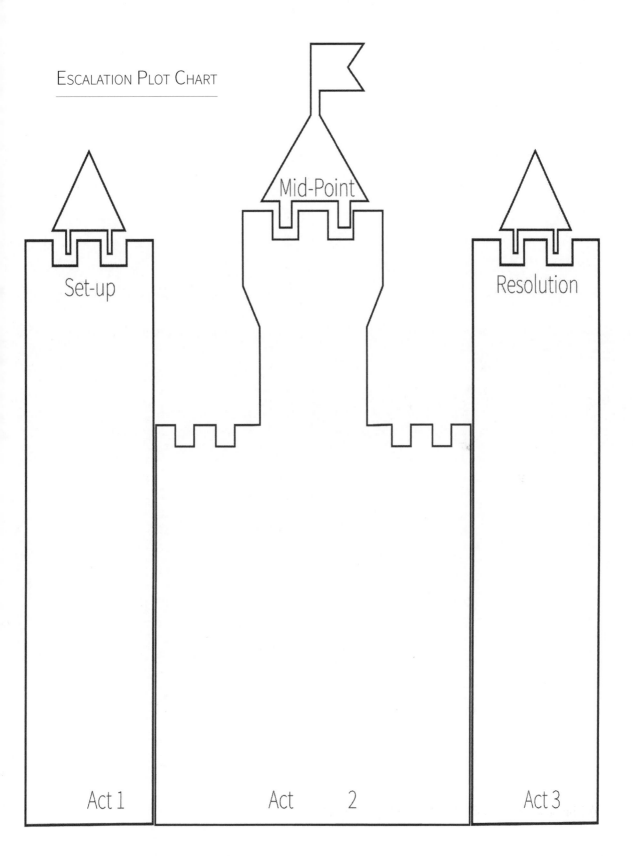

Escalation Plot Chart

Set-up

Mid-Point

Resolution

Act 1

Act 2

Act 3

1.   Focus on your beginning and ending. Do you see the main story thread started in the beginning and wrapped up in the ending?

2.   How well does your beginning introduce the setting, the character, and the conflict?

3.   Do all the story threads get tied up in the end, or do they lead to a sequel? Even if a sequel is on the horizon, is the ending of this story satisfying enough for the reader?

FAIRY TALE MAGIC

Spend some time thinking about the fairy tale magic in your story. Here are some exercises to get you thinking.

1. Who wields the fairy tale magic and how?

2. If you have a magical item, what happens when it falls into the wrong hands? Brainstorm several ideas.

3. How does the fairy tale magic relate to your protagonist? To the stakes in the plot?

4. Keeping the idea of transformation in mind, you can add another layer of depth to your story. How are your characters' inner selves changed by the magic they experience in the plot?

5. What is unique about your fairy tale magic? What is traditional about it?

6. If your fairy tale contains a curse, examine how it works. Who gave it? Have you made the motivation clear, if not right away, by the end of the story?

7. How is your curse broken?

8. Does your fairy tale contain any blessings? Advice or magical items gifted by a wise woman or other fairy tale being? If not, consider adding one.

9. How whimsical is your fairy tale magic? Is there a way for you to make it more so?

THEME

When you've figured out your theme, use this space to plan specific ways to strengthen the theme. Consider all the main sections we've looked at setting, character, plot, and fairy tale magic. How can they be used together to build toward one central theme?

One way to point to theme is to use something called a motif.

You are probably already familiar with the idea of using symbolism in your stories. By extension, a motif is a recurring image that points to and supports the theme. Motifs and symbols are similar concepts; a symbol (representation) is used as a motif when talking about theme.

For example, one reason there are so many royal characters in fairy tales is that they symbolize themes related to power and goodness.

We expect the king to be a wise ruler, honest and fair in his dealings. Likewise, the queen should embody the best of the feminine traits—whether she is ruling the kingdom or managing the household. Therefore, when the royals behave, well, unroyal, we know something has gone very wrong in the kingdom. This makes us cheer for the guileless soldier or simpleton youngest son who outsmarts everyone.

ALLEGORY

Fairy tales, which deal in opposites, are fertile ground for examining faith and values. Good versus evil. Lies versus truth. Moral versus immoral. Heaven versus Hell.

Many of the Grimms' fairy tales are a retelling of the Christian narrative: The Fall, Redemption, and a final judgment leading to destruction for the evil and a Happily Ever After for the righteous.

In an allegory, readers can enjoy the story at face value or dig deeper to reach more layers of understanding. To create a deeper meaning, look for ways to create parallels to the central narrative. Create symbols for what you are trying to represent.

However, keep in mind the limitations of symbols: they represent the thing, but they aren't the thing. Not everything you write in an allegory will match exactly with the underlying story you are trying to mirror, and it's not supposed to. It's more of a parallel than a copy. A way to awaken the moral imagination.

If your story is an allegory, use this space to brainstorm ways to make the connection from a surface story to the deeper story. Consider all aspects of storytelling: character, setting, plot, fairy tale magic, and theme.

TIME TO WRITE YOUR FAIRY TALE

Some authors need only a few key ideas to start writing. Others prefer detailed outlines before they start writing.

Keep experimenting until you find what works best for you. If you've got enough of an idea to get started, start writing. You can add to your notes in this workbook to help keep track of ideas and brainstorm your way out of corners.

WHERE TO GO FROM HERE

If you liked the format of this workbook, there is a companion workbook to *Lessons from Grimm: How to Write a Fairy Tale* which gives less instruction, but more space for brainstorming. It contains enough space to work on three separate tales or a trilogy of fairy tales.

There is also a writing prompts workbook based on Grimms' fairy tales.

*100 prompts: 34 Beginnings, 33 Middles, and 33 Endings

This book is divided into three sections of prompts: Beginnings, Middles, and Endings. Each section works on a different aspect of storytelling and logical thinking. Think of the formula as ABC.

Beginning prompts: Students are given "A" and have to come up with what leads to "B" and "C." Generally, these prompts give characters and setting, but few clues about conflict and plot.

Middle prompts: This type of prompt works on the middle logic of a story. Students are given "B" and have to come up with a logical start "A" as well as a logical conclusion, "C." The conflict is well underway, so they have to unravel what is going on.

Endings: Starting with the conclusion, "C," students work the logic backward to arrive at "A" and "B." Like a detective walking in on a crime scene, they have to come up with characters and motivations and a logical plot that makes sense with the ending.

Appendix: This section lists the story prompt with its original source. Once students have written their stories, they can go and read the Grimms' version and compare ideas.

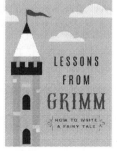
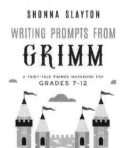
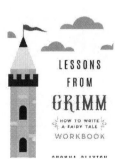

Fairy Tale Archetypes and Tropes

Teachers, if you'd like a separate pdf of the appendix lists found in *Lessons from Grimm: How to Write a Fairy Tale*, go to:

ShonnaSlayton.com/GRIMMpdf/

Here, you can access the link to download Grimms' Fairy Tale Archetypes and Tropes. At the same time, you'll be added to my author newsletter so we can stay in touch.

Also by Shonna

Made in United States
Orlando, FL
09 February 2023

29775267R00041